WORKBOOK

T0346223

Linnette Ansel Erocak • Laura Miller
Series advisor: David Nunan

Pearson Education Limited
Edinburgh Gate
Harlow
Essex CM20 2JE
England
and Associated Companies throughout the world.

Poptropica English

© Pearson Education Limited 2015

Based on the work of Linnette Ansel Erocak

The rights of Laura Miller, and Linnette Erocak to be identified as authors of this work have been asserted by them in accordance with the Copyright, Designs and Patents Act 1988.

Phonics syllabus and activities by Rachel Wilson

Editorial and project management by hyphen

First published 2015
Sixteenth impression 2024

ISBN: 978-1-292-11245-9

Set in Fiendstar 17/21pt

Printed in Slovakia by Neografia

Illustrators: Adam Clay, Moreno Chiacchiera (Beehive Illustration), Chan Sui Fai, Tom Heard (The Bright Agency), Andrew Hennessey, Marek Jagucki, Sue King (Plum Pudding Illustration), Stephanine Lau, Yam Wai Lun, Katie McDee, Bill McGuire (Shannon Associates), Jackie Stafford, Olimpia Wong

All other images © Pearson Education Limited

Every effort has been made to trace the copyright holders and we apologize in advance for any unintentional omissions. We would be pleased to insert the appropriate acknowledgement in any subsequent edition of this publication.

Contents

Welcome

1  **Write. Then match.**

1 _____. I'm Rose.

2 _____. I'm Charlie.

3 _____. I'm Uncle Dan.

4 _____. I'm Ola.

 a

 b

 c

 d

2 **Match.**

1 Hello! I'm Ann. What's your name?

a It's eight o'clock.

2 I'm Sandra. How are you?

b Hello, I'm Peter.

3 Hello, David. What time is it?

c I'm fine, thank you.

Read. Then color.

1 = red	2 = yellow	3 = green	4 = orange
5 = blue	6 = pink	7 = purple	8 = black

 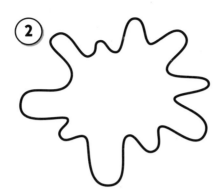

 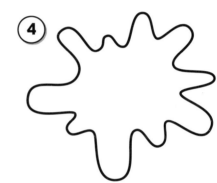

Listen and draw.

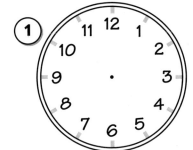

(1)
(2)
(3)
(4)
(5)
(6)

 **Look and write.**

1 What time is it?

It's _____.

2 What _____ is it?

_____

3 What _____ ?

_____

6 Listen and number.

MARKET

OPENS AT 9AM

7 Match. Then number.

wake up

go to bed

eat breakfast

go to school

eat dinner

get up

eat lunch

1

8 Look and write.

1

I _____

at _____ .

2

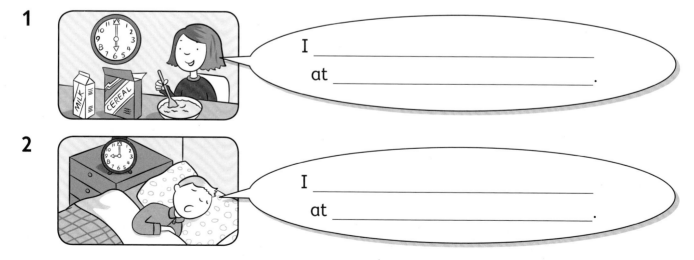

I _____

at _____ .

Unscramble and match. Then draw and write about yourself.

1 gte pu

get up

I _____

at _____.

2 tea dninre

_____

I _____

at _____.

3 og to clshoo

_____

I _____get up_____

at _six o'clock_.

4 eta frbeaakst

_____

I _____

at _____.

5 eta uhlnc

_____

I _____

at _____.

6 og ot deb

_____

I _____

at _____.

 Are you ready for Unit 1?

1 My toys

1 Look and write.

ball   bike   boat   car   doll   kite   teddy bear   train   truck

1

2

3

4

5

6

7

8

9

It's a __boat__.

It's a _____.

It's a _____.

It's a _____.

It's a _____.

It's a _____.

It's a _____.

It's a _____.

It's a _____.

2 Look and circle.

1  (What's / What are) this?
It's a (ball / doll / teddy bear).

2  (What's / What are) that?
It's a (boat / bike / truck).

3  (What's / What are) these?
They're (kite / kites / boats).

4  (What's / What are) those?
They're (bike / truck / bikes).

 3 Listen, count, and color. Then write.

1

2

3

It's a _____

_____ .

They're _____

_____ .

They're _____

_____ .

 **Match.**

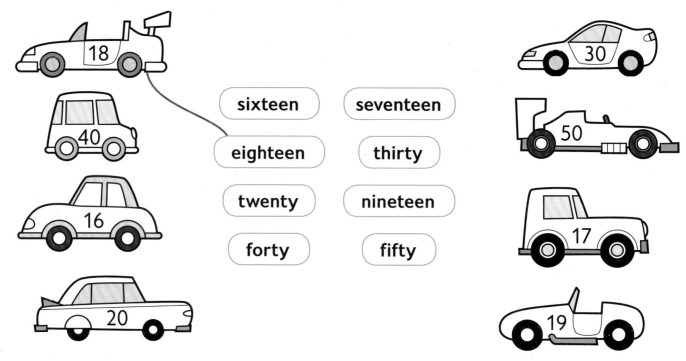

sixteen   seventeen

eighteen   thirty

twenty   nineteen

forty   fifty

5 **Follow the path and count. Then write.**

How many balls are there? There are _____ balls.

Lesson 3   🎧 08 **Sing.** (See Student Book page 14.)

6   **Look, count, and write.**

1

How many _____**bikes**_____ are there?

There are _____**sixteen**_____ bikes.

2

How many _____ are there?

There are _____ dolls.

3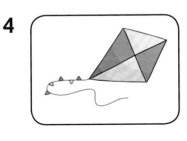

How many _____ are there?

There are _____ boats.

4

How many _____ are there?

There are _____ kites.

7   **Listen and color.**

8   **Look at Activity 7. Write.**

> boat doll kite teddy bear train truck

1 It's a _____.
It's yellow.

2 It's a _____.
It's blue.

3 It's a _____.
It's pink.

4 It's a _____.
It's brown.

5 It's a _____.
It's green.

6 It's a _____.
It's _____.

9   **Look and write.**

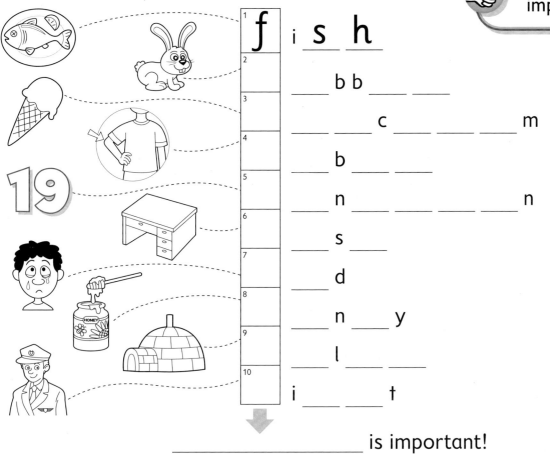

1	f	i	_	s	_	h	_
2		_ _ b b _ _ _ _					
3		_ _ _ _ c _ _ _ _ _ m					
4		_ b _ _ _ _ _					
5		_ n _ _ _ _ _ _ n					
6		_ s _ _					
7		_ _ d					
8		_ n _ y					
9		_ _ l _ _ _					
10		i _ _ _ t					

↓

_____ is important!

10 **Draw two toys you share with friends. Then write.**

I have _____

and _____ .

I share my toys with

_____ and
(name)

_____ .
(name)

(11) **Listen and write.**

(1)   = __4__ dolls

(2)   = _____ trains

(3)      = _____ bike

(4)    = _____ boats

(12) **Match.**

(1)   (a) **20**

(2)   (b) **17**

(3)   (c) **16**

13 Read the words. Circle the pictures.

PHONICS

ch sh

| fish | rich | shell | ship |

14 Listen and connect the letters.

ch   c   h   sh

START   p   f   b   FINISH

s   sh   ch   s

15  Listen and write the words.

1 __ch i n__   2 _____   3 _____   4 _____

16 Read aloud. Then listen and say.

I can see a fish. I can see a shell.

17 **Read and color. Then write.**

It's blue.

It's a _____.

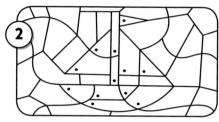

It's yellow.

It's a _____.

It's purple.

It's a _____.

It's green.

It's a _____.

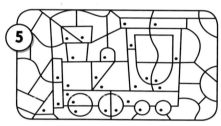

It's orange.

It's a _____.

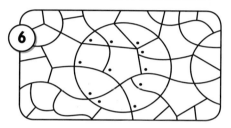

It's pink.

It's a _____.

18 **Look and write.**

What are these?

They're _____.

What are these?

They're _____.

What are these?

They're _____.

What are these?

They're _____.

19 **Look and circle. Then write.**

1

(What's this? / What are those?)
It's a _____ .

2

(What's this / What are these?)
They're _____ .

3

(What's that? / What are these?)
It's a _____ .

4
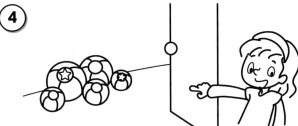

(What's that? / What are those?)
They're _____ .

20 **Read and write. Then draw.**

1 How many balls are there?

There _____ thirteen

_____ .

2 How many kites are there?

There _____ nine

_____ .

 Are you ready for Unit 2?

2 My family

  Look and write.

aunt   cousin   daughter
granddaughter   grandson   son   uncle

This is my dad.

This is my mom.

This is my brother.

This is my cousin.

This is my grandpa.

1   This is my _____.

2   This is my _____.

3   This is my _____.

4   This is my _____.

5   This is my _____.

6   This is my _____.

7   This is my _____.

Look, circle, and write.

| aunt | cousin | granddaughters | grandson |

1

Who's (he / she)?

(He's / She's) my

_____ .

2

Who's (he / she)?

(He's / She's) my

_____ .

3

Who's (he / she)?

(He's / She's) my

_____ .

4

I (have / has) two

_____ .

3 Look and number.

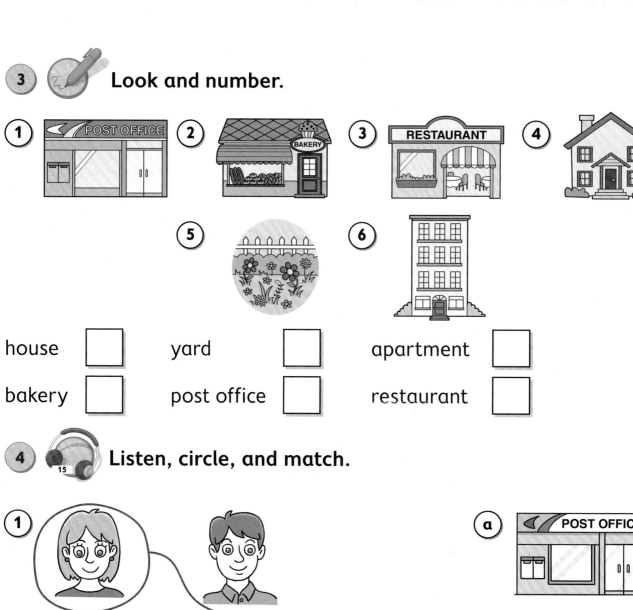

① POST OFFICE   ② BAKERY   ③ RESTAURANT   ④   ⑤   ⑥

house ☐   yard ☐   apartment ☐

bakery ☐   post office ☐   restaurant ☐

4 Listen, circle, and match.

① ② ③ ④

a POST OFFICE   b   c RESTAURANT   d BAKERY

5 Look and write.

apartment bakery house post office restaurant yard

Where's my aunt?

She's in the _____.

Where's my grandson?

He's in the _____.

Where's my granddaughter?

She's in the _____.

Where's my daughter?

She's in the _____.

Where's my son?

He's in the _____.

Where's my uncle?

He's in the _____.

6 Look and number.

 **Read and circle. Then match.**

1 Where is Charlie's grandpa?
He's in the (bakery / store).

 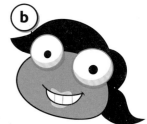

2 Where's Charlie's mom?
She's in the (yard / post office).

3 Where's Charlie's uncle?
He's in the (bakery / yard).

4 Where's Charlie's aunt?
She's in the (store / post office).

8 **What do you like to do with your relatives? Check (✓).**

9 **Draw one of your relatives in your house.**
Then write and circle.

This is my house.

This is my _____.

(He's / She's) in the

_____.

10 **Listen and number. Then write.**

> baby   grandparents   parents   twins

a

☐

_____

b

☐

c

☐

_____

d

☐

_____

11 **Match.**

1    **2**    **3**    **4**

a He's young.   **b** She's young.   **c** She's old.   **d** He's old.

12 Read the words. Circle the pictures.

th th

| math   thick   thin   this |

13  Listen and connect the letters.

(s)   (th)   (th)   (th)

START   (a)   (r)   (s)   FINISH

(th)   (z)   (ch)   (sh)

14  Listen and write the words.

1 _____   2 _____   3 _____   4 _____

15 Read aloud. Then listen and say.

This is a thick book. That is a thin book.

16 **Listen and match.**

1

aunt

2

uncle

3

cousin

4

brother

17 **Look at Activity 16. Circle and write.**

Where's my...?

| apartment   bakery   post office   restaurant |

1 Where's my cousin? (He's / She's) in the _____.

2 Where's my brother? (He's / She's) in the _____.

3 Where's my aunt? (He's / She's) in the _____.

4 Where's my uncle? (He's / She's) in the _____.

18  **Listen and check (✓).**

1

2

3

4

19 **Draw a relative. Then circle and write.**

Where's your _____

_____ ?

(He's / She's) in the

_____ .

⭐ **Are you ready for Unit 3?**

3 Move your body

1 Look and write.

> ~~move~~ nod point shake sit down
> touch turn around wave

 1

_____move_____

2

_____

3

_____

4

_____

5

_____

6

_____

7

_____

8

_____

Look and write.

| arms | body | legs | move | shake | toes | touch | wave |

①

_____ your _____

②

_____ your _____

③

_____ your _____

④

_____ your _____

③   **Listen and number.**

a

b

c

d

4  **Match and write.**

1

2

3

4

5

6

7

8

a ___ ___ the splits

b ju ___ ___

c clim ___

d dan ___ ___

e stand on your h ___ ___ d

f swi _n_ _g_

g do cartwh ___ ___ ls

h swi ___

5 **Look and write. Then circle.**

climb   do cartwheels   do the splits   swim

1

Can you _____ _____ ?

(Yes, I can. / No, I can't.)

2

Can you _____ _____ ?

(Yes, I can. / No, I can't.)

3

Can you _____ _____ ?

(Yes, I can. / No, I can't.)

4

Can you _____ _____ ?

(Yes, I can. / No, I can't.)

6 Match.

1 Jump! Touch your toes!

2 This is fun!

3 Er, can you help? It's the bus.

 **a**

 **b**

 **c**

 7 Circle and number.

 **a**

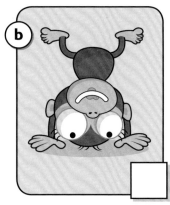 **b**

 **c**

 **d** ☐ 1

1 (Wave / Move) your feet.
2 Stand on your (head / body).
3 (Touch / Wave) your toes.
4 (Move / Nod) your body.
5 (Stand / Shake) on one leg.

 **e**

8 Look and ✓ (= exercise) or ✗ (= not exercise).

9 What exercise do you like? Draw.

10 **Look and write.**

| hop   jump rope   pull   push |

11 **Find and number.**

☐ Wave your arms.

☐ Jump.

☐ Clap your hands.

☐ Touch your toes.

☐ Jump rope.

☐ Hop.

12   **Read the words. Circle the pictures.**

PHONICS

ng   nk

| ink   ring   sing   sink |

13  **Listen and connect the letters.**

| g | nk | ng | c |

START | n | sh | th | FINISH

| ng | k | m | nk |

14 **Listen and write the words.**

1 __ __ __ __   2 __ __ __ __   3 __ __ __ __   4 __ __ __ __

15 **Read aloud. Then listen and say.**

Dad can sing. The girl can sing.

16 **Listen and number.**

17 **Look and write.**

| climb | do the splits | hop | jump rope | swim | swing |

She can _____ .

He can't _____ .

He can _____ .

She can't _____ .

She can't _____ .

He can _____ .

18 **Read and circle. Then say.**

1   Can you stand on your head?   (Yes, I can. / No, I can't.)

2   Can you do cartwheels?   (Yes, I can. / No, I can't.)

3   Can you swim?   (Yes, I can. / No, I can't.)

4   Can you hop?   (Yes, I can. / No, I can't.)

5   Can you climb trees?   (Yes, I can. / No, I can't.)

 Are you ready for Unit 4?

4 My face

1 Look and write.

ears   eyes   face   hair   mouth   nose

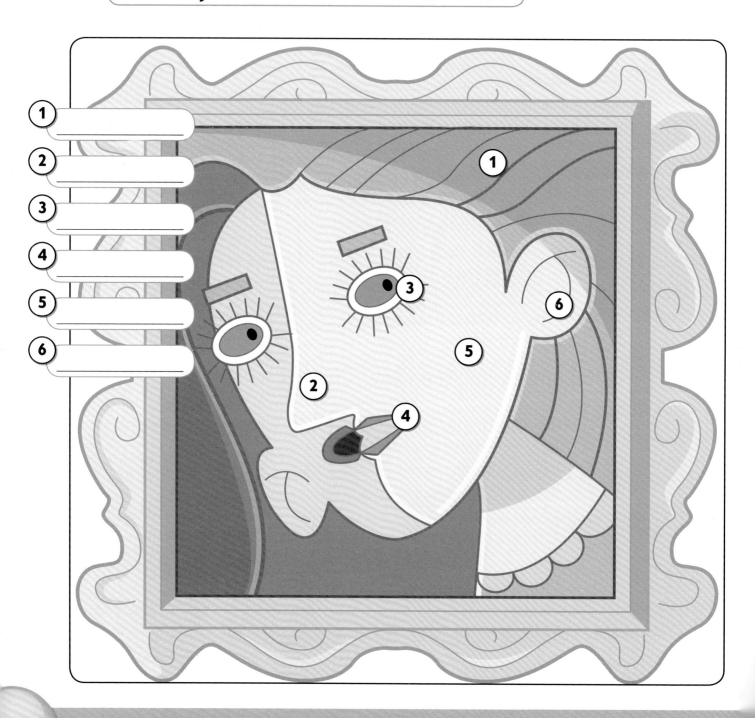

1 _____
2 _____
3 _____
4 _____
5 _____
6 _____

Read. Then look and write 1 or 2.

a   I have big eyes.   **2**

b   I have short hair.   ☐

c   I have a big nose.   ☐

d   I have long hair.   ☐

e   I have small eyes.   ☐

f   I have a big mouth.   ☐

  Look and read. Then circle.

1   Do you have a small mouth?

(Yes, I do. / No, I don't.)

2   Does he have long hair?

(Yes, he does. / No, he doesn't.)

3   Does she have big eyes?

(Yes, she does. / No, she doesn't.)

4   Does he have a small nose?

(Yes, he does. / No, he doesn't.)

Look and circle.

 1   

(long / short) hair

2   

(neat / messy) hair

3   

(short / long) hair

4   

(neat / messy) hair

5   

(blond / dark) hair

6   

(straight / wavy) hair

7   

(dark / blond) hair

8   

(straight / curly) hair

 5    **Listen and check (✓). Then draw.**

☐   big eyes   ☐   small eyes

☐   big nose   ☐   small nose

☐   short, curly hair   ☐   long, straight hair

6 **Listen and circle. Then look and write.**

Grandma   Ruth   Max   Uncle Ed

1 (straight) / wavy / (messy) / blond   It's ___Ruth___.

2 messy / neat / blond / red   It's _____.

3 long / short / straight / curly   It's _____.

4 messy / neat / curly / dark   It's _____.

7 **Look at Activity 6. Choose and write.**

1 Grandma has ___short___ hair.

___Her___ hair is ___dark___ and ___curly___.

2 Ruth has _____ hair.

_____ hair is _____ and _____.

3 Max has _____ hair.

_____ hair is _____ and _____.

4 Uncle Ed has _____ hair.

_____ hair is _____ and _____.

8 **Read and draw.**

He has big eyes.
His mouth is big.
His hair is short.
His hair is neat
and curly.

 9 **Look and write.**

1 She has a _____ nose.

2 _____ has _____ hair.

3 She _____ blond _____.

4 He has _____, _____ hair.

hair
has
he
long
messy
short
small

10 **Listen and ✓ (= likes) or ✗ (= dislikes).**

1

hair ✓   eyes ✓

2

hair   eyes

3

hair   face

4

hair   face

11 **Draw a friend. Then write and circle.**

This is my friend.

(He / She) has _____ eyes

and _____ hair.

12 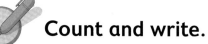 **Count and write.**

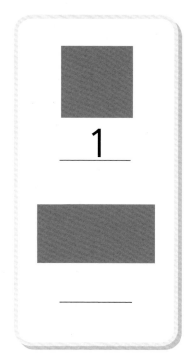

1

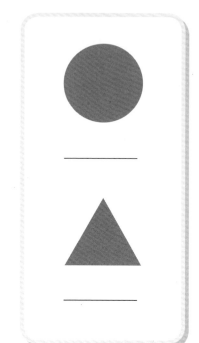

 **13** **Listen, look at Activity 12, and circle.**

1 (Yes / No) **2** (Yes / No) **3** (Yes / No) **4** (Yes / No)

14 **Draw. Use the shapes in Activity 12. Then write.**

It's a _____.

15 **Read the words. Circle the pictures.**

mail   rain   tail   wait

16 **Listen and connect the letters.**

36

ai	e	a	o

START   ee   ai   ee   FINISH

a   u   i   ai

17 **Listen and write the words.**

37

1 __ ____   2 __ ____ __

3 __ ____ __   4 __ __ ____ __

18 **Read aloud. Then listen and say.**

38

The cat has a tail. The cat has four feet.

19 **Listen and color.**

20 **Read. Then look at Activity 19 and circle.**

1 She has big eyes. ((Yes) / No)

2 He has long hair. (Yes / No)

3 She has a small mouth. (Yes / No)

4 He has a small nose. (Yes / No)

5 She has small ears. (Yes / No)

6 He has big ears. (Yes / No)

21 **Look and write.**

1   He has _____ hair.   2   She has _____ hair.

3   He has _____ ears.   4   She has _____ eyes.

5   His mouth is _____.   6   Her nose is _____.

22 **Listen and number.**

 Are you ready for Unit 5?

Lesson 10

49

5 Animals

1 Look and write.

chicken   cow   duck   goat   goose
horse   pig   sheep   turkey

1 _____

2 _____

3 _____

4 _____

5 _____

6 _____

7 _____

8 _____

9 _____

2  **Listen and number.**

a  ☐

b  ☐

c  ☐

d  ☐

3  **Read, look at Activity 2, and write.**

> chicken   curly   duck   feet   goat   legs   sheep   thin

1   What's this?

It has a big mouth and two big _____. It's a _____.

2   What's this?

It has small eyes and a _____ tail. It's a _____.

3   What's this?

It has a _____ body and big ears. It's a _____.

4   What's this?

It has a fat body and black _____. It's a _____.

4 **Look and write.**

bat   crow   fox   owl   skunk

1 _____

2 _____

3 _____

4 _____

5 _____

  5 **Read and match. Then write.**

1 They have big, long tails.
They're brown.

 ⓐ _____

2 They're black and white.
They have long tails.

 ⓑ _____

3 They're thin and black.
They have two legs.

 ⓒ _____

6 **Find and circle. Then write.**

1. Is it small?
2. Are the foxes fat?
3. Is it a crow?
4. Are the skunks thin?

Yes, they are.

No, they aren't.

Yes, they are.

No, they aren't.

Yes, it is.

No, it isn't.

Yes, it is.

No, it isn't.

It's a

_____.

Is it a frog?

_____

They're

_____.

They're

_____.

7 **Read and draw.**

What's that?

1 It's a cow.

2 It's a goat.

3 They're chickens.

4 It's a skunk.

1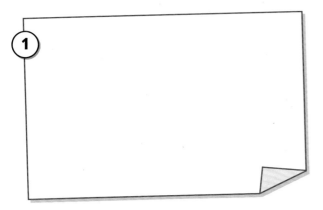

2

3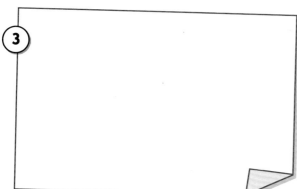

4

8  **Read and match.**

1 It's big. It's black and white.

2 It's thin. It has four legs.

3 They're small. They have wings.

4 It's small. It's black and white.

a

b

c

d

9 **Match.**

1

a

2

b

3

c

4

d

10  **Draw a farm animal you like. Then write.**

It's _____ .

It's _____ .

It has _____ .

It's a _____ .

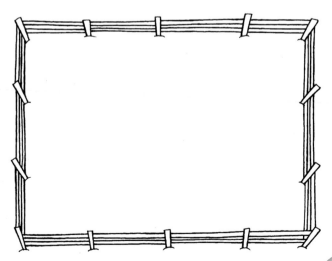

11 Look and write. Then circle.

1  I'm a _____.

I'm (asleep / awake) in the day.

bat
cow
duck
fox
owl

2  I'm a _____.

I'm (asleep / awake) at night.

3 I'm an _____.

I'm (asleep / awake) at night.

4 I'm a _____.

I'm (asleep / awake) in the day.

5  I'm a _____.

I'm (asleep / awake) in the day.

 12 Draw animals from Activity 11.

day

night

13 **Read the words. Circle the pictures.**

boat   goat   light   soap

14  **Listen and connect the letters.**

a	igh		o	a
START	i		oa	FINISH
oa	ch		i	igh

15 **Listen and write the words.**

1 __ ____   2 __ ____   3 __ ____   4 __ ____

16 **Read aloud. Then listen and say.**

The goat has some soap. The goat has a boat.

Where is Uncle Dan?
Listen and follow the path.

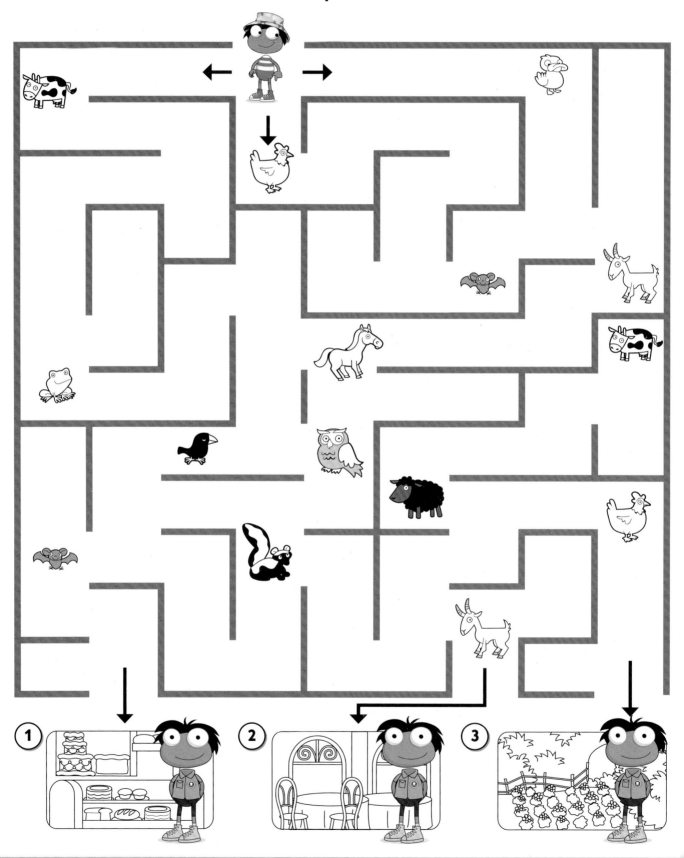

18 **Look, read, and write.**

1 Is the cow big?

   Yes, it is.

2 Are the sheep white?

   _____

3 Is it a chicken?

   _____

   It's an _____.

4 Are they foxes?

   _____

   They're _____.

19 **Listen and check (✓).**

1

   a   b

2

   a   b

3

   a   b

4

   a   b

 Are you ready for Unit 6?

6 Food

1 Look and write. Then draw.

apples   bananas
burgers   chicken
eggs   hot dogs
pizza   rice

1 _____ ✓

2 _____ ✗

3 _____ ✗

4 _____ ✓

5 _____ ✓

6 _____ ✓

7 _____ ✗

8 _____ ✗

2 Look and write.

apples   bananas   chicken   eggs

1   I like _____.

2   I like _____.

3   I like _____.

4   I like _____.

3 Look and circle.

I don't like...

pizza

chicken   hot dogs   rice

apples   burgers   bananas   eggs

4  **Match.**

1

2

3

4

a	grapes	b	toast
c	nuts	d	coconut
e	raisins	f	beans
g	corn	h	pumpkin
i	pineapple	j	cereal

5

6

7

8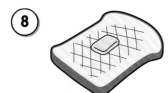

9

10

5  **Look and write.**

My lunch

I like _____, _____, and _____.

But I don't like _____.

6 **Listen and draw.**

1  🙂

2  😐

3  😐

4  😐

5 😐

6  😐

7 **Listen and circle.**

1 She likes ( /  / )

for (breakfast / lunch / dinner).

2 He likes ( /  /)

for (breakfast / lunch / dinner).

3 He likes ()

for (breakfast / lunch / dinner).

4 She likes ()

for (breakfast / lunch / dinner).

8   **Read and draw.**

I like...

apple cake	chicken	apple juice	burgers	bananas

I like...

milk	rice	chocolate cake	banana milkshakes	apples

9   **Draw and write.**

I like _____ for dinner.

I like _____ and rice for dinner.

10 Look and ✓ (= good snacks) or ✗ (= bad snacks).

6

①  ☐

② ☐

③  ☐

④ ☐

⑤ ☐

⑥ ☐

⑦  ☐

⑧  ☐

11  Draw two foods you like and two foods you don't like. Then write.

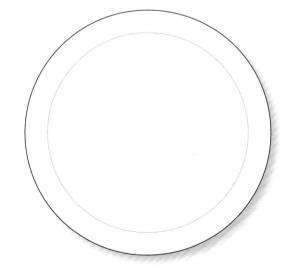

I like _____

and _____.

I don't like _____

or _____.

12 **Read. Then look and number.**

SOCIAL SCIENCE

1 I like tortillas and eggs for breakfast.

2 I like croissants and coffee for breakfast.

3 I like pizza for lunch.

4 I like noodles and vegetables for dinner.

a □   b □   c □   d □

13 **Find and circle.**

E	C	N	C	B	U	R	A	N	P
T	O	A	S	T	V	A	P	I	B
B	P	I	Z	Z	A	I	P	B	A
L	R	L	U	X	A	S	L	U	N
E	B	E	A	N	S	I	E	R	A
C	E	R	E	A	L	N	G	G	N
W	G	R	A	P	E	S	G	E	A
C	H	I	C	K	E	N	B	R	Z
Y	P	U	M	P	K	I	N	N	R

14   **Read the words. Circle the pictures.**

book   foot   look   moon

15  **Listen and connect the letters.**

ee	igh	e	oa

START   a   oo   o   FINISH

oo	ai	ai	oo

16  **Listen and write the words.**

1 _____   2 _____   3 _____   4 _____

17  **Read aloud. Then listen and say.**

Look at the big moon. Look at the book, too.

18   **Listen and circle. Then write.**

I like...
cereal
chicken
pumpkin
beans
apples
corn

I don't like...
toast
pizza
raisins
bananas
eggs
coconut

1   He _____

and _____ .

2   He _____

or _____ .

19  **Listen and draw. Then write.**

_____

_____

_____

_____

20   **Listen and check (✓). Then say.**

1 burgers ☐
apples ☐
chicken ☐
pizza ☐

breakfast ☐
lunch ☐
dinner ☐

2 grapes ☐
nuts ☐
coconut ☐
beans ☐

breakfast ☐
lunch ☐
dinner ☐

3 hot dogs ☐
pizza ☐
corn ☐
grapes ☐

breakfast ☐
lunch ☐
dinner ☐

21 **Draw food. Then write and say.**

She likes _____
and _____
for (breakfast / lunch /
dinner).

 Are you ready for Unit 7?

7 Clothes

1 Find and color. Then write.

dress   pants   shoe   ~~skirt~~   socks   T-shirt

1 an orange ___skirt___   **2** blue _____

3 a pink _____   **4** a red _____

5 a brown _____   **6** green _____

2 🎧 **59** **Listen and check (✓). Then number and color.**

1 purple dress ☐   pink dress ☐   pink skirt ✓

2 black pants ☐   blue pants ☐   brown pants ☐

3 purple skirt ☐   pink skirt ☐   purple dress ☐

4 brown shoes ☐   red socks ☐   red shoes ☐

☐   ☐   **1**   ☐

3 🖌️ **Read and color. Then look and write.**

blue

red

orange

green

brown

yellow

1 I'm wearing _____ shoes and a _____ skirt.

2 I'm wearing a _____ T-shirt and _____ pants.

3 I'm wearing a _____ dress and _____ socks.

Look and write.

Vacation Clothes

boots	cap	coat
jeans	pajamas	shirt
sneakers	sweater	

1. _____

2. _____

3. _____

4. _____

5. _____

6. _____

7. _____

8. _____

5 Listen and look. Then circle.

1

(Yes, I do. / No, I don't.)
I want (red shorts / red pants).

2

(Yes, I do. / No, I don't.)
I want (a pink boot / pink boots).

3

(Yes, I do. / No, I don't.)
I want (a yellow shirt / a yellow skirt).

4

(Yes, I do. / No, I don't.)
I want (a blue pajamas / blue pajamas).

6 Listen and match. Then color.

Find and color. Then write.

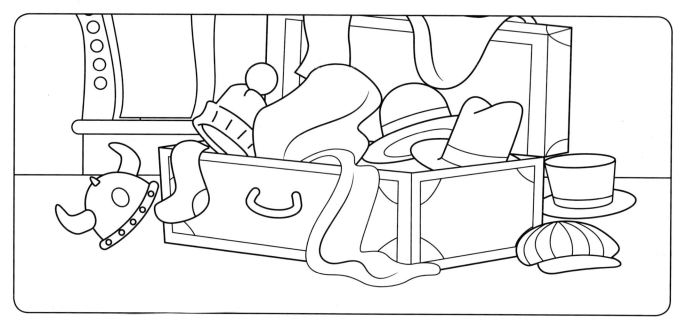

There are _____ hats.

8 **What's missing? Draw and write.**

1 I'm wearing a _____ _____ .

2 I'm wearing a _____ _____ .

9  **Look and write.**

> **Good morning!   Good night.   Goodbye!**
> **I'm sorry.   Please.   Thank you.**

1 _____

2 _____

3 _____

4 _____

5 _____

6 _____

10  **Draw. Then circle and write.**

It's time for _____.

(Put on / Take off)
your _____.

11 **Look and write.**

| chef | firefighter | nurse | police officer |

I'm a _____.

I'm a _____.

1

2

3

4

I'm a _____.

I'm a _____.

12 **Read. Then look at Activity 11 and number.**

a I'm wearing a shirt, black pants, and black shoes. I'm wearing a hat. ☐

b I'm wearing a white dress, a hat, and black shoes. ☐

c I'm wearing a coat and boots. I'm wearing a helmet. ☐

d I'm wearing a T-shirt and pants. I'm wearing white shoes and a tall hat. ☐

13 **Read the words. Circle the pictures.**

ar	ir
or	ur

car   girl   shark   surf

14  **Listen and connect the letters.**

ir	or	ur	r

START   o   ck   or   FINISH

ar	ai	ch	ar

15  **Listen and write the words.**

1 ___ ___   2 ___ ___   3 ___ ___ ___   4 ___ ___

16 **Read aloud. Then listen and say.**

See the girl surf. See the shark surf!

17 Look and write.

bed   boots   pajamas   pajamas
school   shoes   sweater   T-shirt

1

Take off your _____.

2

Put on your _____.

3

Put on your _____.

4

It's time for _____.

5

Take off your _____.

6

Take off your _____.

7

Put on your _____.

8

It's time for _____.

18   **Read and number. Then color.**

1 I'm wearing yellow pajamas.

2 I'm wearing red shoes.

3 I'm wearing black boots.

4 I'm wearing blue pants.

19 **Write. Then listen and draw.**

67

| boots | dress | hat | pants | shoes |
| skirt | socks | sweater | T-shirt |

1

2

3

I'm wearing
a ___dress___,
a _____,
and _____.

I'm wearing
a _____,
a _____,
and _____.

I'm wearing
a _____,
_____,
and _____.

 Are you ready for Unit 8?

8 Weather

  Look and write. Then read and circle.

| cloudy | cool | rainy | snowy | sunny | windy |

It's _____sunny_____.

Is it rainy?

(Yes / No)

It's _____.

Is it cloudy?

(Yes / No)

It's _____.

Is it sunny?

(Yes / No)

It's _____.

Is it windy?

(Yes / No)

It's _____.

Is it cool?

(Yes / No)

It's _____.

Is it snowy?

(Yes / No)

2 **Write the days of the week.**

1 S _ _ _ _ _ _   2 M _ _ _ _ _ _   3 T _ _ _ _ _ _ _

4 W _ _ _ _ _ _ _ _ _   5 T _ _ _ _ _ _ _ _   6 F _ _ _ _ _ _

7 S _ _ _ _ _ _ _ _

3 **Listen and write. Then draw.**

| cloudy | cool | rainy | snowy | sunny | windy |

1 I like _____ days.

2 I don't like _____ days.

3 I like _____ days.

4 I don't like _____ days.

5 I like _____ days.

6 I don't like _____ days.

4 **Look and write.**

| fly | go | make | read | ride | take |

1 _____ a snowman

2 _____ for a walk

3 _____ a bike

4 _____ a picture

5 _____ a kite

6 _____ a book

5  **Listen and match.**

1 Monday   **a** rainy

2 Thursday   **b** sunny

3 Saturday   **c** windy

4 Tuesday   **d** stormy

6   **Read, look, and write. Then number.**

1 What's the weather like?

_____ windy.

_____ day is it today?

It's _____ .

2 What's the weather like?

_____ cool.

_____ day is it today?

It's _____ .

3 What's the weather like?

_____ sunny.

What _____ is it today?

It's _____ .

4 What's the weather like?

_____ cloudy.

What _____ is it today?

It's _____ .

Sunday	Monday	Tuesday	Wednesday	Thursday	Friday	Saturday
□	□	□	□	□	□	□

7 **Listen and write. Then draw.**

Friday	Saturday	Sunday	Monday

It's _____ . It's _____ . It's _____ . It's _____ .

8 **Listen and number. Then match.**

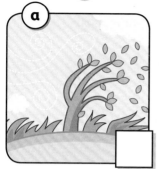 a

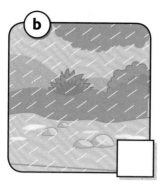 b

 c

 d

 **9** **Find and write.**

1	2	3	4	5	6	7	8	9	10	11	12	13
a	b	c	d	e	f	g	h	i	j	k	l	m

14	15	16	17	18	19	20	21	22	23	24	25	26
n	o	p	q	r	s	t	u	v	w	x	y	z

‾‾ ‾‾ ‾‾ ‾‾ ‾‾ ‾‾ ‾‾ ‾‾ ‾‾ ‾‾ ‾‾ ‾‾ ‾‾ ‾‾ ‾‾ ‾‾ ‾‾ ‾‾ ‾‾!
23 5 12 3 15 13 5 20 15 25 15 21 18 16 9 3 14 9 3

VALUES

 10 **Look and check (✓) what you share with other people.**

Share with friends and family.

	Friends	Sister(s)	Brother(s)	Parents

11 **Draw two things you share with friends and family. Then write.**

I share _____
and _____
with my friends and family.

12   **Look and write. Then listen and number.**

cold   freezing   hot   warm

a

_____

b

_____

c

d

13 **Look and write. Then draw.**

It's sunny.

It's _____.

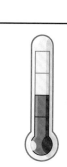

It's windy.

It's _____.

It's cloudy.

It's _____.

It's snowy.

It's _____.

14   **Read the words. Circle the pictures.**

ow   oy

boy   cow   cowboy   down

15  **Listen and connect the letters.**

ar	o	h	w

START   j   oy   oy   FINISH

ow	y	p	ow

16 **Listen and write the words.**

1 _____   2 _____   3 _____   4 _____

17 **Read aloud. Then listen and say.**

The boy watches the cowboy. The cow watches the boy.

18   **Read and look. Then write 1 or 2.**

Picture 1

Picture 2

a It's cloudy. `1` **b** I'm wearing a T-shirt and pants. ☐

c I have a train. ☐ **d** I like pizza. ☐

e I'm wearing a dress. ☐ **f** I don't have a doll. ☐

g I like chicken. ☐ **h** Look at my dog. It's big. ☐

i It's sunny. ☐ **j** I'm wearing boots. ☐

8

19 **Read and number. Then write.**

cloudy   snowy   sunny   windy

a   He's in the yard.

It's _____. ☐

b   I'm wearing big boots!

It's _____. ☐

c   She has a bike.

It's _____. ☐

d   I'm wearing a sweater.

It's _____. ☐

20 **Draw yourself. Then write.**

1   I'm wearing _____

_____.

2   I like _____.

3   I don't like _____.

4   I have _____

_____.

Goodbye

1 Look and write.

castle   cave   clothes   dinner
doctor   farmer   mountain   shopping

1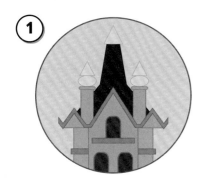

Help at the _____.

2

Help with _____.

3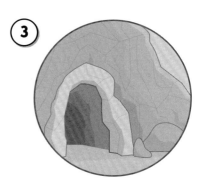

Help at the _____.

4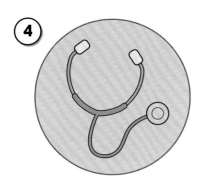

Help the _____.

5

Help the _____.

6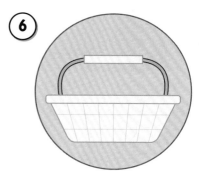

Help with the _____.

7

Help with the _____.

8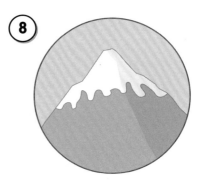

Help at the _____.

Circle. Then look and write.

1  Where (is / are) the grapes?

The _____ the refrigerator.

2  Where (is / are) the duck?

The _____ the sink.

3  Where (is / are) the pants?

The _____ the bed.

4  Where (is / are) the hat?

The _____ the cow.

3 **Listen and check (✓).**

1

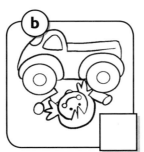

2

3

4

1 Where <u>are the shoes</u>? <u>They're in the tub</u>.

2 Where _____?

_____.

3 _____?

_____.

4 _____?

_____.

5 **Draw these five things in the living room. Then write.**

ball   book   boots   shorts   teddy bear

1   The boots _____.

2   The ball _____.

3   The book _____.

4   The shorts _____.

5   The teddy bear _____.

Structures

Welcome

> **What time is it?**
> **It's** one **o'clock**.

> I **wake up at** six **o'clock**.

Unit 1 My toys

What's this/that?	**It's a** bike. **It's** yellow.
What are these/those?	**They're** bikes. **They're** yellow.

> **How many** bikes **are there?**
> **There are** sixteen bikes.

Unit 2 My family

Who's he/she?	**He's/She's my** uncle/aunt.
	Who's = Who is

Where's my uncle?	**Your** uncle **is in the** house.
Where's your uncle?	**My** uncle **is in the** house.

Unit 3 Move your body

Touch your toes.

| Can you jump? | Yes, I can. / No, I can't. |
| Can he/she jump? | Yes, he/she can. / No, he/she can't. |

Unit 4 My face

I have a small nose.	He/She has a small nose.
Do you have a small nose?	Yes, I do. / No, I don't.
Does he/she have a small nose?	Yes, he/she does. / No, he/she doesn't.

He/She has long hair.

His/Her hair is long.

Unit 5 Animals

| What's this/that? | It has big eyes. It's black and white. It's a cow. |

| Is it small? Is it a bat? | Yes, it is. / No, it isn't. |
| Are the bats big? | Yes, they are. / No, they aren't. |

Unit 6 Food

What's your favorite food?	**My favorite food is** pizza.
I like chicken.	**I don't like** eggs.

He/She	likes	pineapple for breakfast.
	doesn't like	
Does he/she like pineapple for breakfast?	Yes, **he/she does**.
	No, **he/she doesn't**.

Unit 7 Clothes

I'm wearing a white skirt.
I'm not wearing white pants.

What do you want?	**I want** a shirt, please.
Do you want a blue shirt?	Yes, **I do**. / No, **I don't**. **I want** a red shirt.

Unit 8 Weather

Do you like cloudy days?	Yes, **I do**. / No, **I don't**.
I like cloudy days.	**I don't like** cloudy days.

What day is it today?	**It's** Sunday.
What's the weather like?	**It's** sunny.